Pianoworks

BOOK 1

Janet and Alan Bullard

MUSIC DEPARTMENT

OXFORD
UNIVERSITY PRESS

Great Clarendon Street, Oxford OX2 6DP, England
198 Madison Avenue, New York, NY, 10016, USA

Oxford University Press is a department of the University of Oxford.
It furthers the University's aim of excellence in research, scholarship,
and education by publishing worldwide

12

ISBN 978–0–19–335582–8

Music and text origination by
Barnes Music Engraving Ltd., East Sussex.
Printed in Great Britain on acid-free paper by
Halstan & Co. Ltd., Amersham, Bucks.

Image of digital piano supplied courtesy of Roland.
Image of grand piano and upright piano supplied courtesy of Steinway.
Line drawings by Richard Corfield

All pieces are original compositions or arrangements by the authors unless otherwise stated.

The authors would like to thank all the teachers, pupils, and friends who
have tried out the contents of this book, for their helpful comments and
advice, and also the editorial team at Oxford University Press for their
consistent encouragement and help.

Preface

Congratulations on taking that first step towards piano playing with *Pianoworks 1*!

There are many reasons for wanting to learn the piano. Whatever your aims, you will find playing the piano a fulfilling and absorbing activity, which not only keeps your fingers supple but also keeps your brain active.

Unlike many books for beginner pianists, the Pianoworks series is designed for anyone, of whatever age, who prefers a more adult approach to their learning—who knows what they want to achieve but needs some help along the way. By working through *Pianoworks 1* and *Pianoworks 2* (forthcoming) you will develop the skills necessary to play piano pieces of all styles, from the great works of the past to the music of today.

Pianoworks 1 is suitable for complete beginners and those with some past experience who feel they would like to 'start again'. It aims to be methodical, developing your musical skills by giving clearly focused information, with every new idea defined and explained; an index is provided for quick reference. The book contains more than forty pieces, including a mix of carefully arranged classical and traditional works and new compositions—each chosen to reinforce the technical points made. Pianoworks is based on the traditional concept of learning to play from written music—a good background for playing all types of music—but also includes extra work in listening, playing by ear, and using the piano creatively.

To help you with your studies, the accompanying CD includes each piece recorded as a solo, so you can hear what you are aiming for. For many of the pieces, there is also a special piano accompaniment you can play along with. The CD also includes some opportunities to play by ear and improvise.

Although the book contains all the information you need to make a good start on playing the piano, for best results we recommend that you work through it with an experienced piano teacher, as only in this way can you develop according to your individual needs.

You will find that regular practice is the best way to make progress. Why not put aside 15 to 30 minutes every day as your special practice time? This is so much better than a large chunk of practice once or twice a week.

Thirty more pieces, from medieval to modern, are included in the *Pianoworks Collection Book 1*. This is an excellent way to build on the skills learnt in this book.

Good luck, and enjoy your piano playing!

JANET AND ALAN BULLARD

Contents

Your piano

This book is suitable for anyone learning on a traditional piano, either upright or grand, or on a digital piano with full-size keyboard (88 notes) and keys that are weighted and touch-sensitive. It is not suitable for electronic keyboards without these qualities, which require a different playing technique.

If you do not have a piano, please take specialist advice in choosing one. It's worth remembering two points:

- 'Real' pianos, both grand and upright, depreciate in value more slowly than electric ones, but they need regular tuning and servicing, and cheap 'bargains' may not work well enough for you to achieve your best. In good condition, though, they have more subtlety of tone, and most pianists find them more rewarding to play.

- Electric digital pianos (provided they are touch-sensitive and with weighted keys) have many advantages in smaller houses, but they lose their value quickly and never quite have the same feel or sound as a real piano. However, most of them can produce considerably better results than a worn-out upright, and headphones can keep the neighbours (or your family) happy!

How the piano works

Strings, keys, and hammers

Look inside an upright or grand piano and you will see metal strings stretched across an iron frame. Behind the frame (on an upright piano) or beneath it (on a grand) is a wooden **soundboard** which amplifies the sound. Most of the strings are grouped in threes, and each set of three strings is tuned to the same pitch. At the left hand side of the piano the lower strings are grouped in pairs, and the lowest and thickest strings have just one string for each pitch. The strings are attached to **tuning pegs** which can be turned to adjust the pitch of each string, although this skilled job should be left to a piano tuner.

Press a key on the keyboard while looking inside, and you'll see that it does two things:

- it causes the **hammer** to hit the string (or group of strings) and bounce off, resting a small distance away. (The hammer is below the string on a grand piano and in front of it on an upright.)

- it makes the **damper** move away from the string, allowing the string to vibrate. (The damper is above the string on a grand and in front of it on an upright.)

If you press the key with more force or weight, the hammer hits the string more quickly and makes a louder note.

When you let go of the key:

- the hammer falls back to its original position.

- the damper moves onto the string, making the sound stop.

Pedals

Most pianos have two pedals; try pressing them, looking inside while you do so.

- The **sustaining pedal** (on the right) moves the dampers away from the strings so that the strings continue to vibrate after you let go of the key—this enables the performer to produce a richer and fuller sound. If you see just the word 'Pedal', this is the one it means.

- The **soft pedal** (on the left) makes the sound quieter. On a grand it does this by moving the keyboard along a little so that only one string of each group is struck (it just strikes the edge of the single strings), and on an upright it moves all the hammers a little nearer to the strings.

- Some small uprights have a middle 'practice pedal', which dampens and quietens the sound; and some concert grands have a middle 'sostenuto' pedal. This is rather like the sustaining pedal, but it sustains only the notes that are in use when it is pressed, and not any that may be played subsequently; it is rarely called for.

Electronic pianos

Good electronic pianos are designed to feel and sound as much like an acoustic piano as possible. The sound of the grand piano is sampled digitally and the pedals and keys are intended to feel like 'the real thing', so that, in theory, there should be no difference in the technique required to play them.

Starting to play

Sitting at the piano

If you have an adjustable piano stool, place it centrally and about a foot away from the edge of the keyboard, so that you can sit comfortably on the front part.

Adjust the height of the stool so that when you place your hands on the keys, your elbows are slightly higher than the keyboard—you will find it easier if you take your weight off the stool while you adjust it.

If your stool is not adjustable, and is not the right height, try placing a book or cushion on it. If you sit on a chair with a back, do not be tempted to lean against it.

Relax!

You will get much better results in your piano playing if you are relaxed. Always do some relaxation exercises before you start to play. You may have your favourites, or you could try these:

- Let your arms fall loosely by your side with shoulders and elbows relaxed, breathing slowly and regularly.

- Gently roll your shoulders in a circle to release any tension.

- Slowly rotate your head in a half-circle from side to side (*never* a full circle) to keep your neck muscles relaxed.

Hands, fingers, and thumbs

Unlike many other keyboard instruments such as the organ or harpsichord, the piano is designed so that you can play quietly, loudly, and with all the shades of expression in between simply by using your fingers. This control can best be achieved with curved fingers rather than flat ones, as in the picture below. Notice how you will be playing on the side of the thumb and the pads of the fingers.

- With your hands in this rounded shape, and with relaxed shoulders and elbows, flop your hands onto the keys and bounce off again, moving to different parts of the keyboard—don't worry about the strange sounds!

- Now try playing with just the middle finger on different parts of the keyboard, right hand then left hand, keeping the same feeling of relaxed bouncing that you did when flopping your hands.

- Now flop your hands onto the keyboard, with the fingers and thumb spaced evenly above five white keys ready to play them—this is called the **'five-finger' position**.

- Notice how the sound that you make responds very sensitively to your **touch**—the way that you press the key.

- Always make sure that the elbows are relaxed to avoid a harsh tone quality.

Fingering

In piano playing, the fingers and thumbs are numbered from 1 to 5 in each hand: the thumb is number 1, and the little finger is number 5.

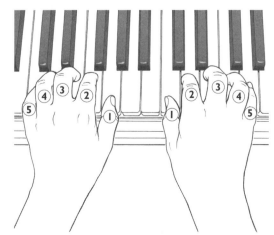

Seven letters for seven notes

In music, the first seven letters of the alphabet are used to name the notes—A, B, C, D, E, F, G, then back to A again. The notes go from left to right on the keyboard, as you can see in the diagram on pages 12 and 13. The further to the right you go, the higher in **pitch** the notes become, and as you move to the left the notes become lower. The distance between one note and the nearest note with the same name is called an **octave**.

The five-finger position: left hand

Find all the Cs on your piano. C is the note immediately to the left of each group of two black notes. On most pianos there are seven or eight of them. Using the third (or middle) finger of your left hand, play each one in turn, starting with the lowest.

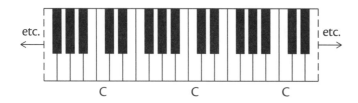

Middle C is the C nearest to the centre of the keyboard; it is shaded in grey in this keyboard diagram.

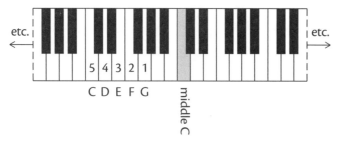

- With shoulders and arms relaxed, place your fifth (or little) finger of your left hand on the C an octave below middle C, with your other fingers and thumb resting lightly on D, E, F, and G (the white notes immediately to the right), as in the diagram.

- Remember to keep your fingers slightly curved.

- Keeping your hand in this position, play each note in turn, at a steady and even pace, moving smoothly up from C to G and down again. There should be no break between the notes. Lift one finger as the next is lowered, as if you were walking on the keys. ⊙ **track 1** demonstrates how it should sound.

- When you are confident with this and can play evenly and steadily, try playing the same finger pattern but starting on other notes. Listen to the effect. For example, try putting the fifth finger on D (one note to the right of C) or on E (one note to the right of that).

- Now you could try making up your own tunes, using just the five notes covered by your hand.

You may well find it hard to play evenly, so if you feel your hand or body getting tense, do the relaxing exercises on page 8, or go and have a cup of coffee!

Remember that the best way to develop your skills is 'little and often'.

The five-finger position: right hand

- Find all the Cs on your piano, and this time play them with the third finger of your right hand.

- Now place your right hand thumb on middle C, with your other fingers resting on D, E, F, and G (the white notes immediately to the right).

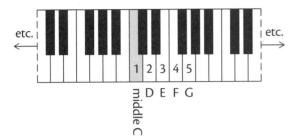

- Remember to keep your fingers slightly curved, and your shoulders and arms relaxed.

- Keeping your hand in this position, play each note in turn, at a steady and even pace, moving smoothly up from C to G and down again. **track 2**

- Try starting on different notes (e.g. on D or E) as you did with the left hand.

- If you like, make up your own tunes as well.

On the CD are some more exercises to help you with finding your way around the keyboard and with note names.

Sit at your piano and listen to **track 3**.

Reading music

So far we've managed without having to read music, but that bridge will have to be crossed very soon. On the next two pages are the basic facts about how music is written down. If you can read music already, you can skip these pages; if it's all rather new to you then please read them, but don't worry if it doesn't all make sense at first as the main points will be explained again in later pages.

Musical notation

Pitch

Piano music is written on two **staves**, joined together with a **brace**. Each stave (or staff) consists of five lines, and the notes are placed on the lines and in the four spaces between them. Lines and spaces are numbered from the bottom upwards. The position of the notes relative to the stave indicates their pitch.

The upper stave is for the right hand, playing the higher notes, and usually uses a **treble clef**.

The lower stave is for the left hand, playing the lower notes, and usually uses a **bass clef**.

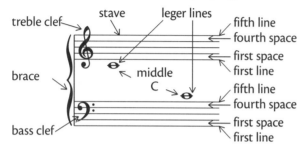

The easiest way to work out the names of the notes and their position on the keyboard is to start with middle C—the nearest C to the middle of the keyboard (remember that C is the note immediately to the left of each group of two black notes). Middle C is notated on an extra line, called a **leger line**. Depending on which hand is playing it, it is just below the treble (right hand) stave or just above the bass (left hand) stave. You can see this in the diagram above.

All the other white notes on the keyboard can be worked out starting from middle C. As the treble clef notes move upwards to higher pitches (i.e. to the right of the keyboard) you move forwards through the seven-note musical alphabet (C, D, E, F, G, A, B). As the bass clef notes move downwards to lower pitches, you move backwards through the seven letters.

The black notes help you to find your bearings: just as C is always the note to the *left* of the group of two black notes, D is always *between* the two black notes, and E is always to the *right* of them. F, G, A, and B can be similarly identified by their position relative to the group of *three* black notes. For the moment, don't worry about the names of the black notes—these will be explained on page 32.

The diagram below shows the whole keyboard and where each of the white notes appears on the staves. Middle C is shown twice—once for each hand—although it is the same note on the keyboard. The less frequently used notes (the really high and low notes at the far ends) are not notated here.

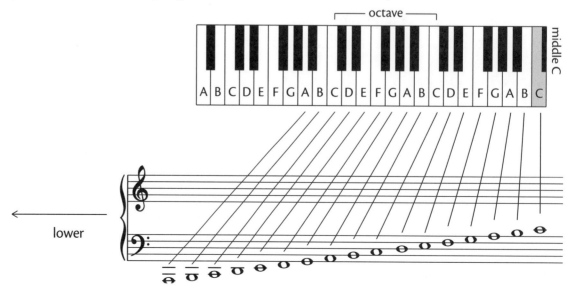

Rhythm

The shape of a note indicates its length, and therefore the **rhythm**, by showing how many beats (or counts) each note lasts for. All except the semibreve have a **stem** which points up or down depending on the position of the note on the stave, but the direction of the stem makes no difference to the length of the note.

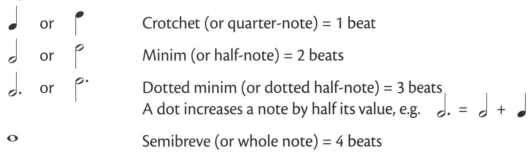

Crotchet (or quarter-note) = 1 beat

Minim (or half-note) = 2 beats

Dotted minim (or dotted half-note) = 3 beats
A dot increases a note by half its value, e.g.

Semibreve (or whole note) = 4 beats

Music is usually divided into **bars** (or **measures**), indicated by a vertical **bar-line** through the stave. The end of a piece of music is indicated by a **double-bar**. In this book, **bar numbers** are placed at the beginning of the second and subsequent staves. These do not affect the performance but are purely for reference.

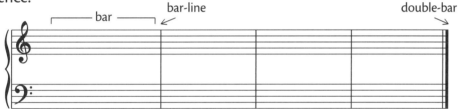

The **time signature** shows how many beats there are in each bar or measure:

- The top number tells us how many **beats** to count.
- The bottom number (4) tells us that we are counting crotchets or quarter-notes.

Here are some frequently used time signatures with the correct number of notes in each bar.

two crotchet beats per bar

three crotchet beats per bar

four crotchet beats per bar

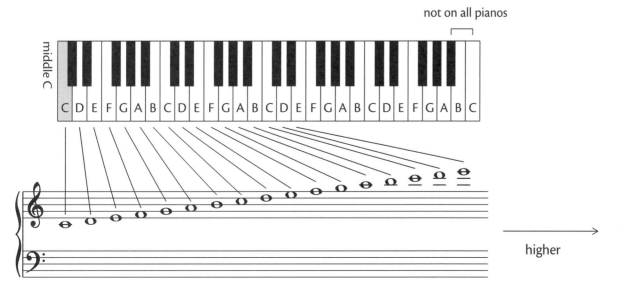

Pulse and rhythm

All music has a steady sense of forward direction—the feeling of 'keeping going'. This is achieved by a sense of pulse and rhythm.

Pulse

The pulse is the regular beat which enables the music to move forward in time. Often thought of as 'counting' (e.g. 1, 2, 3, 4, 1, 2, 3, 4), this is the backbone of the music, though not usually heard out loud. The Italian word **tempo** is used when referring to the speed of the pulse.

Rhythm

Whereas you count the pulse in your head, the rhythm is what you actually play. So, before you play a new piece, make sure that you understand the rhythm. A good way to practise this is to count the pulse steadily out loud, and tap or play the rhythm at the same time.

- Listen to the click of the pulse and the rhythm (on the piano) on **track 4**.

- Notice how in the pulse there is a slight emphasis or **accent** on each of the 'one's. This accent marks the first beat of each bar.

Here is the same exercise in rhythmic notation—the vertical lines indicate the beginning of each bar.

- Try clapping or playing the rhythm yourself (pick any note), counting the pulse out loud at first, and then in your head.

- Don't fall into the trap of stopping when you see a bar-line, or at the end of a line of music!

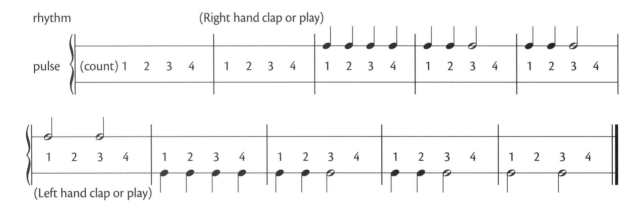

Both pieces on the next page use the rhythm you have practised above, but with different hand positions to achieve contrasting moods.

- The keyboard diagrams show the hand position required for each piece. In both, the first note is played with the thumb (see the little '1' above the note) beginning with the right hand.

- Relax your arms, and get both hands in position over the notes with the fingers curved.

- Follow the direction of the notes to read the melody—on this page they always move to the next note up or down except for the last note in each hand.

Sorrowful should be played more slowly (at a slower tempo) than *Joyful*. Note that whilst the *rhythm* is the same, the *pulse* is slower, but still regular. It's quite hard to count a slow pulse at first; make sure you don't get faster!

On the CD you will find recordings for each of the pieces in the book: **Solo** shows how you should sound, and **Duet** is another piano part that you can play along with, like a backing track.
On some tracks there is a two-bar 'count-in' of clicks, to indicate the pulse.

🔘 **track 5** Solo
🔘 **track 6** Duet

Joyful

Moderate speed

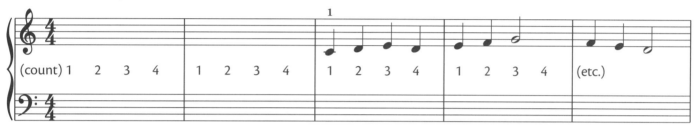

🔘 **track 7** Solo
🔘 **track 8** Duet

Sorrowful

Slowly

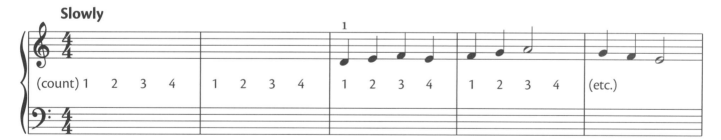

Time signatures

The pieces you have played so far have had four crotchet beats in a bar, and the pulse has been in crotchets (quarter notes), hence the $\frac{4}{4}$ time signature.

$\frac{4}{4}$ is sometimes abbreviated to **C** (**common time**).

In $\frac{3}{4}$ the first of every three crotchet beats is slightly accented.

Count 1-2-3 1-2-3.

You often find ♩. (dotted minim/dotted half-note) in $\frac{3}{4}$; it lasts for three beats.

In $\frac{2}{4}$ the first of every two crotchet beats is slightly accented.

Count 1-2 1-2.

Approach the pieces on the next two pages as follows:

- Find out how many beats there are in the bar from the top number of the time signature.
- Count the pulse regularly—either 1-2-3-4 1-2-3-4, 1-2-3 1-2-3, or 1-2 1-2, depending on how many beats there are in the bar, slightly accenting the 'one' each time.
- Tap the rhythm while you count the pulse in your head.
- Using the keyboard diagram as a guide, place your hands in the correct hand position and rest your fingers lightly above the keys, ready to play.
- Keep counting the pulse steadily while you play.
- Follow the line of the notes as they rise and fall on the stave. In these pieces there are more leaps, but you never have to move your hand, so use the position of your thumb as an anchor.
- Move your fingers steadily and evenly. As you press each key release the previous one to produce a smooth musical flow, like walking.
- You may find it helpful to break the piece into sections and practise them separately. The final aim is to get to the end without stopping, but this will probably take several attempts, so don't give up!

🔵 **track 9** Solo
🔵 **track 10** Duet

Dance

Susato
16th cent.

Rhythmically

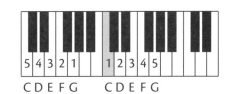

🔵 **track 11** Solo
🔵 **track 12** Duet

A Hurried Conversation

Quite fast

track 13 Solo
track 14 Duet

The First Waltz

Steady and flowing

track 15 Solo
track 16 Duet

Evening Calm

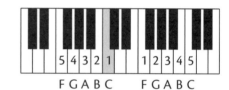

Smoothly and steadily

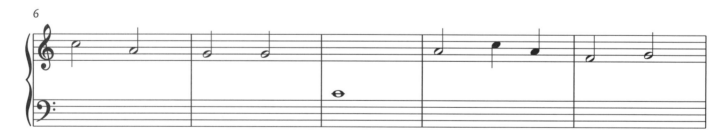

Note and rhythm check-up

Notes

- Say the alphabet out loud from A to G.

- Say the alphabet *backwards* from G to A.

- Starting on any A, and using the third finger of either hand, play the white notes upwards, stopping when you get to G. Say the names of the notes as you play them.

- Do the same, but start on any G, moving downwards and stopping when you get to A.

- Play all the Ds on your piano, starting with the lowest.

- Play all the Fs, starting with the highest.

- Play all the Gs, starting with the lowest.

See how quickly you can play and name these notes:

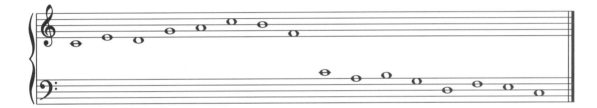

Rhythm

Clap or play the following rhythms. Before you start, check the time signature, then count two bars of pulse in your head (or out loud), and keep counting while you clap the rhythm.

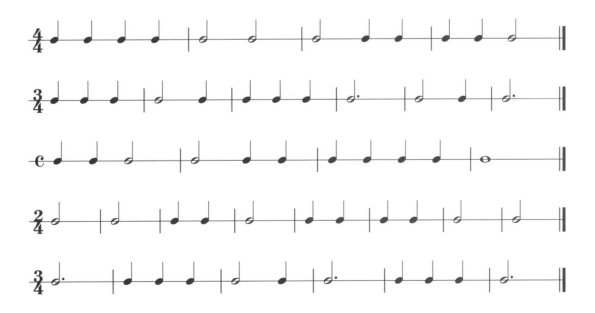

Legato and staccato

These Italian words describe the *articulation* of a melody—whether it is played smoothly (*legato*) or detached (*staccato*). They do not affect the rhythm of the melody, but they do affect the length that you hold the note on for.

Legato

Listen to track **17**.

Notice how the piano simulates the effect of a smooth, singing musical line. One finger comes up exactly as the next one goes down, like a see-saw, to make a continuous musical flow.

Most music is flowing and legato in character, but often legato playing is specifically indicated by a curved line (or *slur*) above or below the notes. Each note within the slur should move smoothly to the next, as if in one breath. Try this for yourself, playing with both hands in turn.

Staccato

Listen to track **18**.

Each note (except the last) is short and crisp, with a gap between each note—but the actual rhythm is the same as the legato exercise above. The hand and fingers bounce up slightly between each note, as if you were tapping with your fingertips. Keep your wrist loose and relaxed.

Staccato playing is indicated by a dot above or below each note. Try this, again playing with both hands in turn.

In the pieces that follow, practise making the legato melody flow between the hands where marked by the slur. Always count steadily so that the speed remains the same, whether staccato or legato. *Good King Wenceslas* needs a new hand position in which both thumbs share middle C. Keep your fingers curved over the keys and keep the thumbs raised when not playing so that they don't get entangled with each other!

track 19 Solo
track 20 Duet

Sharing a Tune

Gently

track 21 Solo
track 22 Duet

Good King Wenceslas

Piae Cantiones (1582)

Joyfully

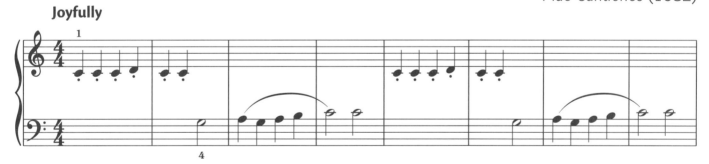

Rests

The **rest** is used to indicate a silence. Each note length has a corresponding rest:

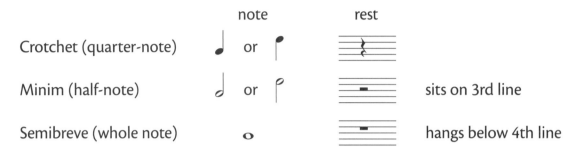

	note	rest	
Crotchet (quarter-note)	♩ or ♩	𝄽	
Minim (half-note)	𝅗𝅥 or 𝅗𝅥	▬	sits on 3rd line
Semibreve (whole note)	𝅝	▬	hangs below 4th line

The semibreve rest is also used for a whole bar of silence, whatever the time signature.

Clap or play the following rhythms, counting in two bars before you start. You can hear them played on 🔊**track 23**.

The next two pieces both contain rests. *Five-finger Rag* uses rhythms characteristic of the American ragtime style developed in the late nineteenth century. Ragtime is short for 'ragged time', achieved by the rest on the third beat of the bar.

- Both pieces have the same hand position as *Good King Wenceslas*, so keep the thumbs raised when not playing.

- As always, count steadily; although the music may appear to stop where there's a rest, the pulse must keep going regularly.

23

🎵 **track 24** Solo
🎵 **track 25** Duet

Footsteps

Creepily

dying away to the end

🎵 **track 26** Solo
🎵 **track 27** Duet

Five-finger Rag

Loud and rhythmic

Quavers

The **quaver** (or eighth-note) lasts half the length of a crotchet (quarter-note).

When two (or more) quavers follow each other, they are sometimes joined together by a **beam**. This has no effect on the lengths of the individual quavers.

Clap or play the following rhythms. Remember that the pulse is still a crotchet in length, and so it helps to count 'and' for the quavers. You can hear these played on ⊙ **track 28**

Count: 1-and-2-and - 1-and-2-and

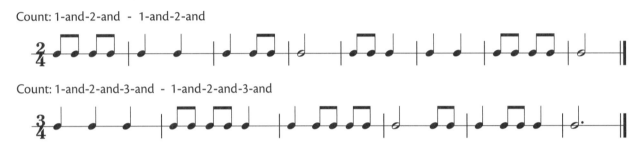

Count: 1-and-2-and-3-and - 1-and-2-and-3-and

The Irish Lady is an old folk dance which was first published in a collection of over 500 traditional tunes called *The Dancing Master*. This was published, in several volumes, by the father-and-son team John and Henry Playford in the second half of the eighteenth century.

 **track 29** Solo
⊙ **track 30** Duet

The Irish Lady

Anon.
Playford's *The Dancing Master*

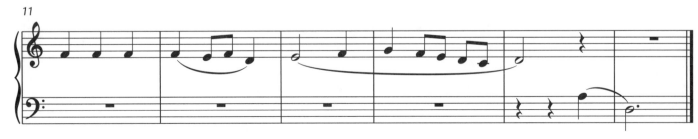

Accents

The sign $>$ is an accent, and indicates that you should play the note more forcefully.

In this short exercise, emphasize the accented notes, but do not play them harshly; relax the tension as soon as the note has been struck. Listen to ⊙ **track 31** to hear how this should sound.

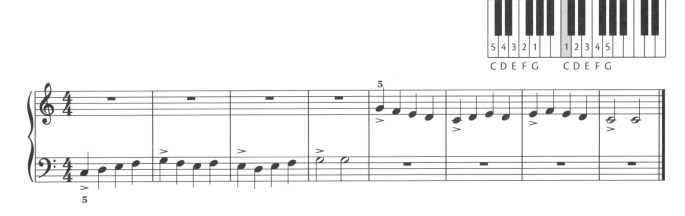

African Song uses 'call and response', typical of African work songs and of the blues—a leader sings a phrase, and everyone else echoes it. Traditional sailors' songs or 'shanties' were a European equivalent.

⊙ **track 32** Solo
⊙ **track 33** Duet

African Song

Firmly and detached

Call and response exercises

On ⊙ **track 34–8** are some more call and response exercises for you to try. Just follow the instructions on the CD.

Hands together

The following three examples will help you develop good coordination when playing with both hands at the same time. You can hear them on ☉ **track 39**.

- Practise each hand separately first, and when you feel secure, play with both hands together.

- Don't forget to count the pulse in your head to keep the rhythm steady.

In the first exercise the two hands are playing the same pattern of notes, but mostly moving in opposite directions. This is called **contrary motion**.

In the next two exercises the hands are moving in the same direction. This is called **similar motion**.

In the next exercise your LH thumb is playing the D above middle C, which sits above the middle C leger line

In the following pieces, practise each hand separately (rhythm first, then with the notes), then play with hands together. Remember to count steadily as you play, always moving forward.

Aim for a smooth legato in *Winter*, and a bright, clear sound in *Summer*.

Winter

Steadily

Welsh folk tune

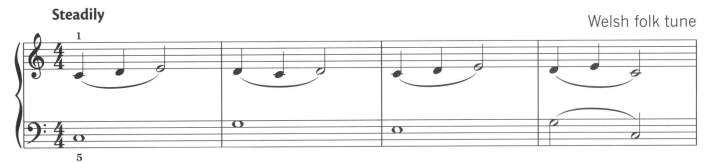

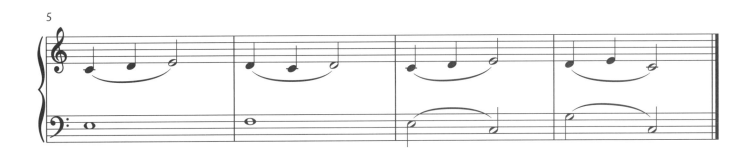

Summer

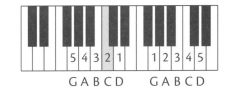

Joyfully

Repeat marks

The repeat mark :‖ means repeat from the beginning, or from the previous ‖:

So, in *Autumn*, the whole piece is repeated, and in *Spring*, each line of music is repeated in turn.

Autumn has a calm and gentle sound, with the main melodic idea flowing from hand to hand. In *Spring*, the legato sections contrast with a bouncy and lively staccato. Try playing the repeats more quietly the second time, as on the CD.

Upbeats

Not all pieces start on the first beat of the bar; they often start on the last beat. This is called an **upbeat** or **anacrusis**. When this happens, the last bar is shortened by one beat to compensate.

The English folk song *Strawberry Fair* starts with an upbeat. Count in like this: 1-2-3-4 1-2-3-(play). The lines between the staves indicate that the melody moves from hand to hand. You'll notice that the quavers here are sometimes linked in groups of four—this makes no difference to the length of the notes.

🔘 **track 48** Solo   **Strawberry Fair**

Dynamics

We use the word **dynamics** to refer to the loudness and quietness with which you play. There are two basic dynamic markings, and like many musical words, they are in Italian.

f (*forte*) means play loudly (with more arm weight, but never with too much force)
p (*piano*) means play quietly (with less arm weight, but still with good tone)

Most other dynamic markings are variants of these:

mf (*mezzo-forte*) means moderately loud, not as loud as *f*
mp (*mezzo-piano*) means moderately quiet, not as quiet as *p*
ff (*fortissimo*) means very loud
pp (*pianissimo*) means very quiet

cresc. (*crescendo*) or ───────── means gradually getting louder

dim. (*diminuendo*) or ───────── means gradually getting quieter

Practise these exercises, hands separately and then together, grading the tone gently from one dynamic to the next, and keeping the arms relaxed.

🔘 **track 49**

🔘 **track 50**

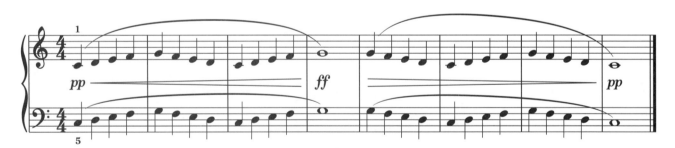

In *Echo Song*, emphasize the contrasts between *forte* and *piano* to highlight the echo effect.

Imagine a slowly moving procession of camels in *Desert Song*, with the *crescendos* and *diminuendos* suggesting the ongoing journey.

🎵 **track 51** Solo

Echo Song

DEFGA   DEFGA

Cheerfully

Folk tune from Cyprus

🎵 **track 52** Solo
🎵 **track 53** Duet

Desert Song

EFGAB   EFGAB

Steadily

Accidentals

Accidentals are the signs that go before a note to change its pitch.

Sharp (♯)

A sharp before a note raises it to the very next note above (a **semitone** higher)—this is usually the black note just above it (i.e. to the right). The sharp applies to any subsequent notes at the same pitch in the same bar.

Here are some short melodies for each hand using sharps:

- Make sure that your fingers are curved and well forward over the keys, so that you can easily cover the black notes as well as the white.

 track 54

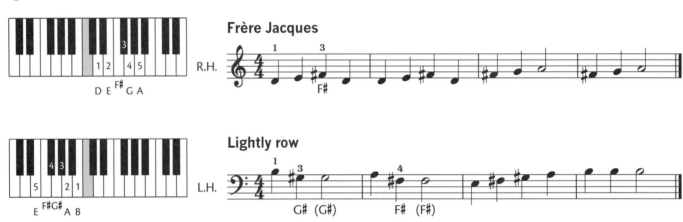

In the lively *Fiesta* place the third fingers over F sharp in both hands before you start.

Flat (♭)

A flat before a note lowers it to the very next note below (a semitone lower)—this is usually the black note just below it (i.e. to the left). As with the sharp, it applies to any subsequent notes at the same pitch in the same bar.

- In these short melodies, remember once again to keep your fingers well forward.

🔘 **track 57**

The flattened Bs help to give an air of calmness to *Siesta*. Again, make sure that your fingers are in place over the black and white keys.

🔘 **track 58** Solo
🔘 **track 59** Duet

Siesta

More on sharps and flats

Every black note on the piano has two names. For example, B flat is the same as A sharp. You can see this in *Travelling Blues* on page 51.

Natural (♮)

A natural cancels any previous sharp or flat and restores a note to its normal pitch. In the example below, the naturals cancel out the sharps that have appeared earlier in the bar.

🔘 **track 60**

Cautionary accidental

An accidental lasts only for the remainder of the bar in which it occurs. However, it is often useful to be reminded that a note has now returned to its normal pitch, as in the example below. These reminders are called cautionary accidentals; sometimes they appear in brackets, but this doesn't mean they are optional!

🔘 **track 61**

In *Changing Moods*, you will hear how the C sharp gives a brighter sound to the phrase, whereas the C natural creates a more melancholy character.

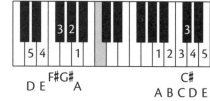

🔘 **track 62** Solo

Changing Moods

Playing through, practising, and performing

Often when you want to get to know a new piece, you might play it through as best you can without stopping to correct mistakes. That's fine, but if you want to learn a piece properly then you need to practise it, and practising is not the same thing as playing the piece over and over again.

Here are some tips on how best to structure your practice sessions:

- Before you start to practise, relax, with the routine on page 8.

- Then warm up by playing exercises like the ones on pages 26 and 30.

- You are now ready to start work on your new piece, and you should begin by working with hands separately. Often you will need to work on a section at a time, depending on the length of the piece.

- First work out the rhythm, then the notes and fingering; finally, check for any detail such as staccato marks or dynamics.

- Play any problem areas over and over again until you are confident with them, and only then play the section or the whole piece right through in time.

- If anything goes wrong, try to see *why* it went wrong and focus on that area—don't keep going back to the beginning. Successful practice depends on analysing the difficulty and finding a solution to it.

- When you are confident with each hand separately, practise the piece with hands together. You might stumble at first, and you will need to practise some sections many times. Again, don't keep going back to the beginning (you can probably play the first bar). Find where the problem is, and work on that tricky passage, hands together, but just two or three notes at first, gradually extending the passage in both directions until it is happily under your fingers.

- 'Practice makes perfect' is a cliché, but it's true!

To finish your practice session, it's a good idea to relax by performing a favourite piece that you already know well. Performing is again different from practising or playing through: begin by thinking yourself into the mood and speed of the piece, then once you've started playing keep going in time, even if you make a mistake. Whether anyone is listening or not, imagine you have an audience: they won't want to hear you go back and try again!

Speed indications

Traditionally, speed indications (or tempo markings) are given in Italian. Here are some of the most common markings used, some of which you will come across in the pieces that follow:

Presto – very fast
con moto – with movement
Allegro – fast and lively
Allegretto – quite fast but not as fast as Allegro
Moderato – moderate tempo
Andante – at a walking pace (medium tempo)

Adagio – slow
Lento or **Largo** – very slow
ritardando, rit. – getting gradually slower
accelerando, accel. – getting gradually faster
a tempo – back to the previous tempo/speed

Ties and dots

Ties

When two notes of the same pitch are joined together with a curved line (known as a tie), the second note is not sounded—in effect the two notes are added together.

A good way to practise tied notes is to play them without the ties first. Try this with the following exercise:

🔵 **track 63** (without ties and then with ties)

Don't confuse the tie with the *slur* (page 20) which is used to indicate legato. The tie is placed next to the note-heads; the slur is usually placed over or under notes of different pitches and is further away from the note-heads.

Dots

You've already met the *dotted minim*. The dot, placed immediately after the note, adds half the length of the note to it, so that the two beats of the minim become three beats in total. In effect, the dot is used in place of a tie:

Try the two exercises below; they sound the same, though they are written differently.

🔵 **track 64**

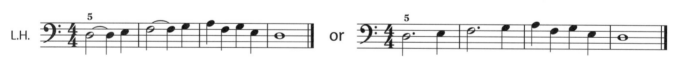

The American spiritual *When the Saints Go Marching In* uses ties and dotted minims. Always count the pulse carefully.

Where's the keyboard diagram gone?

You've just seen your last keyboard diagram. Now that you are more confident with note reading you can find the hand position for each piece without one. Look at the fingering for the first note in each hand, find the notes on the keyboard, and place your hands in the correct position.

When the Saints Go Marching In

Allegro   American spiritual

More dots

The same rule applies to the *dotted crotchet* as to the dotted minim: to the crotchet (one beat) we add a quaver (half a beat): ♩. = ♩ ♪

Think of them as tied notes, and count 'and' for the quavers (as on page 24).

🔘 **track 67** (without ties and then with ties)

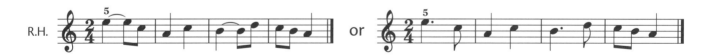

🔘 **track 68** (without ties and then with ties)

The Welsh folk tune *All Through the Night* and the Irish *Cockles and Mussels* both use dotted crotchets. In *All Through the Night* the melody is shared between the hands; following the dynamic markings will help the melody to sing through.

🔘 **track 69** Solo

All Through the Night

Welsh folk tune

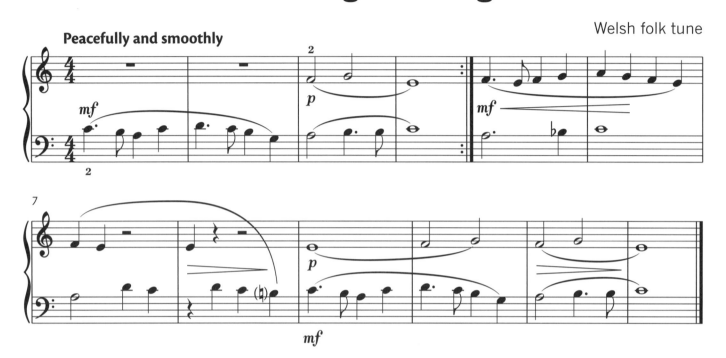

🔘 **track 70** Solo

Cockles and Mussels

Irish folk tune

Note and rhythm check-up

Notes

Using the third finger of either hand:

- play all the B flats on the piano, starting with the lowest.
- play all the F sharps, starting with the highest.
- play all the C sharps, starting with the lowest.

See how quickly you can name and play the notes below:

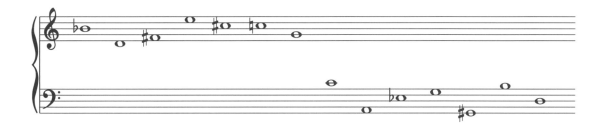

Rhythm

Clap or play the following rhythms. Before you start, check the time signature, then count two bars of pulse in your head, and keep counting while you clap the rhythm.

Call and response exercises

On 🔘 **tracks 71– 4** are some more call and response exercises for you to try. Just follow the instructions on the CD.

Beyond the five-finger position

In everything that you've played so far, your fingers have remained next to each other, in the five-finger position. Most music uses more than five notes, so here are some exercises to get your fingers moving beyond the five-finger position.

Practise playing each exercise below legato and staccato (as on page 20), taking each hand in turn.

First and second fingers

After playing each thumb note, position the second finger on the next note but one. Keep repeating the pattern until the thumb comes round to C again.

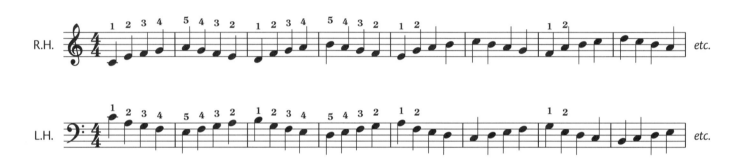

First and fifth fingers

Keep the hands relaxed while rotating the wrists gently with a rocking movement as you move from one note to the next.

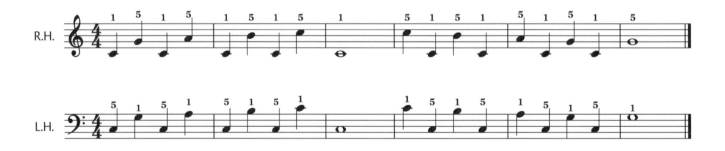

When learning *Pendulum*, begin (as always) with hands separately. Practise the quaver passages slowly, rotating the wrists gently, and making sure that the rhythm is completely even.

track 75 Solo

Pendulum

J. B.

Moving hand positions

This exercise will help you to become comfortable with moving from one hand position to another.

- Jump gently from one hand position to the next.
- Practise hands separately first, and then together.

The next two pieces both use moving hand positions. The fingering is marked only where the hand moves. You might find it helpful to pencil in an upward or a downward arrow on the music to remind you where to move. (By the way, don't be embarrassed about writing reminders on your music—most pianists do this!)

🔘 **track 76** Solo

Swaying Pines

A. B.

Andante

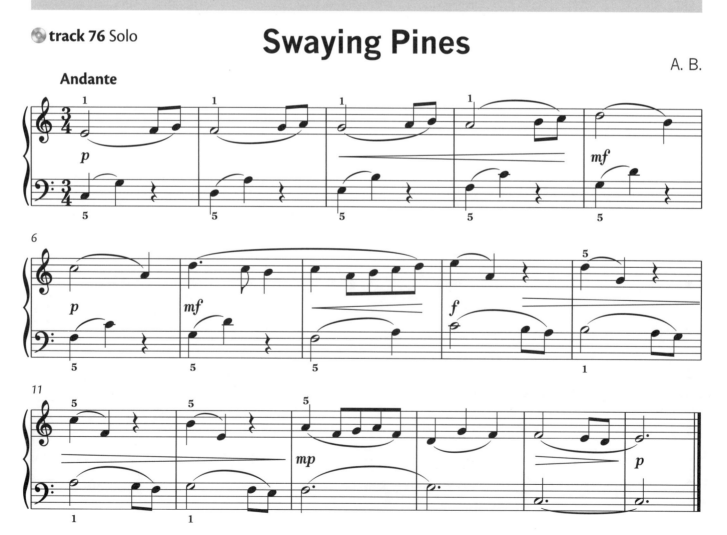

track 77 Solo

Highland Games

J. B.

Chords

track 78

A *chord* is two or more notes played simultaneously.

- Practise the following hands separately and then together, with a relaxed and bouncing wrist.

- Aim for an even tone in this next exercise, and make sure the notes of each chord sound exactly together.

- Note that when two notes are adjacent, as in the first bar, they are not printed directly above each other as there isn't room. They must still be played simultaneously.

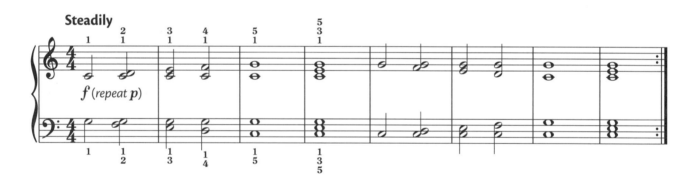

- In these legato chords, make sure the fingers go down together.

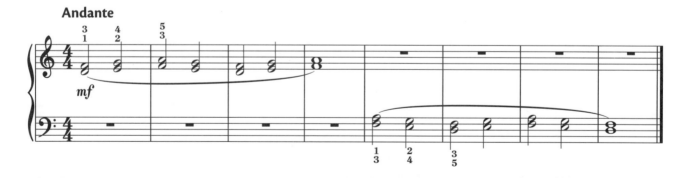

The exercise above helps to prepare you for the *Chord Study* by Ferdinand Beyer (1803–63), taken from his *Elementary Method of Piano Instruction*.

Moving further back in time, *Ungaresca* is a piano arrangement of a medieval Italian dance intended to represent the sound of Hungarian bagpipes. Aim for a lively and bright sound here: crisp staccato crotchets will help create the dance-like effect.

track 79 Solo

Chord Study

Ferdinand Beyer
(1803–63)

track 80 Solo
track 81 Duet

Ungaresca

Anon.
16th cent.

Sustaining Pedal

The sustaining pedal is the pedal to the right (on pianos with three pedals, the furthest to the right). It is the most used pedal and is sometimes called the 'damper pedal', but more often simply the 'pedal'.

- If you have a traditional upright or grand, look inside the piano and press the pedal down—the dampers all move away from the strings. This means that when you play a note, the strings continue to vibrate even when you let go of the note, and the sound is sustained.

As well as sustaining the sound, the pedal also enriches it, giving a new dimension to the musical colour.

- Hold the pedal down with your right foot, and with any fingers play a series of *black* notes.
- Notice how the pedal sustains the sound and creates a rich texture.
- Play the following patterns with the pedal held down:

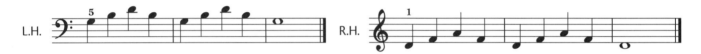

- Notice how the pedal creates a chord from the individual notes.

Using the pedal

- Keeping your heel on the floor, raise and lower the pedal with the ball of your foot. Keep your foot in contact with the pedal all the time so that it moves smoothly and noiselessly.

The sign below indicates the use of the pedal. Press the pedal down at *Ped.* and raise it at the end of the bracket.

Ped.⎤

- Play the following exercises, counting in time while you raise and lower the pedal.

lift pedal on '3'

| 1 | 2 | 3 | 4 | 1 | 2 | 3 | 4 | 1 | 2 | 3 | 4 | 1 | 2 | 3 | 4 |

Ped.⎤ Ped.⎤ Ped.⎤ Ped.⎤

lift pedal on '4'

| 1 | 2 | 3 | 4 | 1 | 2 | 3 | 4 | 1 | 2 | 3 | 4 | 1 | 2 | 3 | 4 |

Ped.⎤ Ped.⎤ Ped.⎤ Ped.⎤

- Here are some exercises to coordinate the left hand and the pedal.

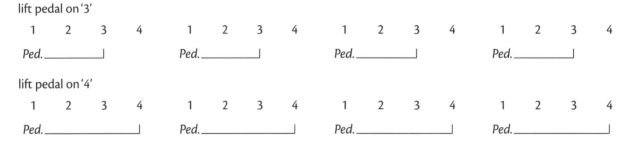

Mystical Memories uses mostly black notes which, together with the pedal, create a rich sonority. Place your hands well forward, with fingers slightly further apart than normal, so as to cover the notes easily. Practise it without the sustaining pedal first, then play it with the pedal as marked, listening carefully to the sound.

track 82 Solo

Mystical Memories

A. B.

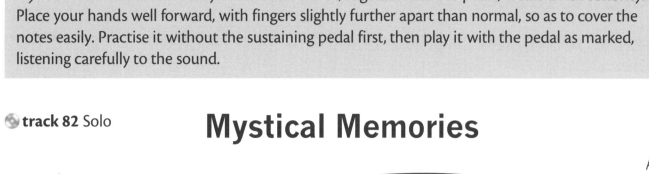

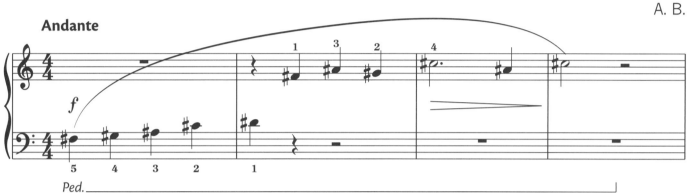

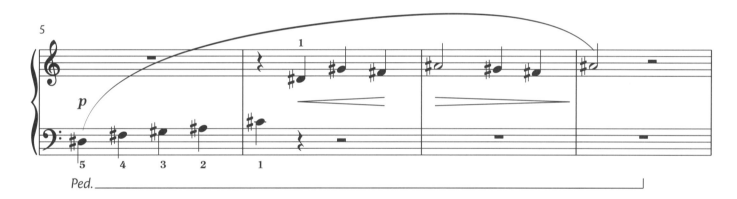

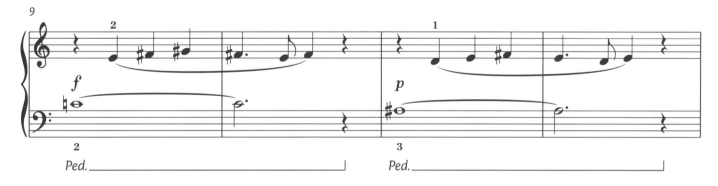

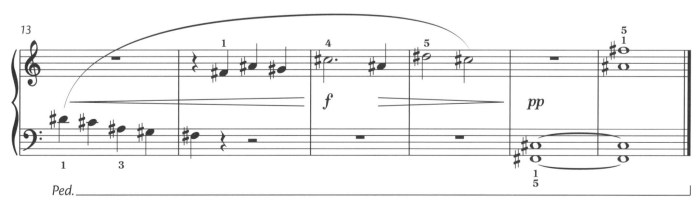

More notes

We've already met some notes using leger lines:

Here are all the notes using single leger lines above and below the stave, preceded by the nearest note without a leger line:

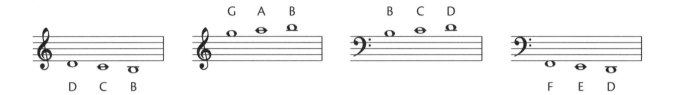

When the music goes higher or lower, more leger lines are added. In effect, leger lines simply extend the stave to more than five lines. To work the notes out, just continue to name them in order, up or down the scale.

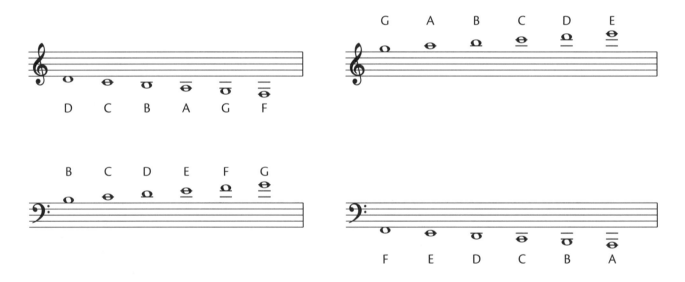

Sometimes different clefs are used to avoid too many leger lines. The examples below both sound the same, but in the second one the left hand notes are written in the treble clef to avoid using lots of leger lines.

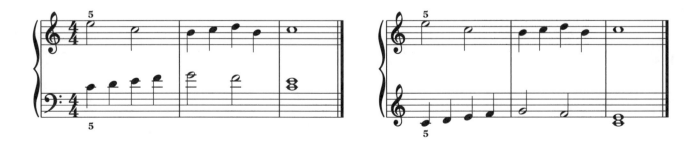

Crossing hands

So far, you have moved only a short distance from one hand position to the next. Here are some exercises to help you cover a wider range by crossing one hand over the other—aim to keep your shoulders relaxed as you move into the new position.

In this exercise the left hand travels over the right hand, ready to play the top Cs, which are written on the upper stave. Start to move the left hand slowly into position as you play the right hand notes.

track 83

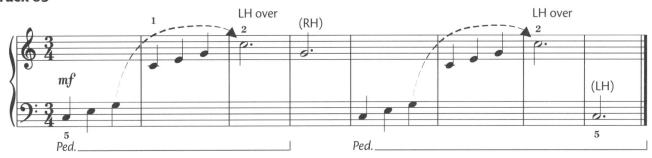

Here, the right hand moves over the left hand, to play the same phrase two octaves lower. Note the change from the treble to the bass clef in the RH part.

track 84

Overleaf are two pieces using some of the techniques you have recently learned.

In *Shoreline*, the crescendos and diminuendos will help you play with lots of expression. Make the hands cross over smoothly (look out for clef changes), and listen carefully to the sound, always raising the pedal where marked. 'Rit.' (short for ritardando) means gradually getting slower—the emphasis is on the gradually, so not all at once! This is a good piece to play from memory when you have got to know it.

Play the lively *Travelling Blues* with exuberance and tight rhythm. Make a clear contrast between the different dynamics, and at the half-way point use the rests to get the left hand into the new position. This piece uses the traditional twelve-bar blues chord scheme (twice) and the characteristic 'out-of-key' feel of the blue note (B flat/A sharp).

Senza Ped. means without pedal.

track 85 Solo

Shoreline

J. B.

🔘 **track 86** Solo

Travelling Blues

A. B.

Scales, tones, and semitones

A **scale** is the name given to the sequence of notes between one letter name and the next occurrence of the same letter name.

A scale can start on any note, and it is made of a series of **intervals** (the distance between one note and the next) called tones and semitones.

A **semitone** is the distance between two notes next to each other, including black notes; a **tone** (or whole tone) is two semitones.

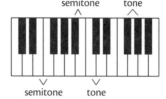

There are a number of different types of scale, and the most common is the *major* scale, in which the semitones and tones are always arranged in this pattern:

tone tone semitone tone tone tone semitone (t t s t t t s)

This means that if you start a major scale on C, you are playing in the **key of C major** which uses only the white notes—a good place to start!

C major scale

Scale playing is a good opportunity to use the 'thumb under' technique. Before tackling the complete scale, play this exercise, hands separately, with the fingering shown. To help the thumb swing gently under the fingers, keep your fingers curved and not too near the edge of the keys, allowing your wrist to move flexibly rather than letting your elbow swing outwards. Repeat the exercise until you are comfortable with this movement.

Now play the complete C major scale, each hand in turn:

and now with the same fingering, but with the left hand going up and then down:

The First Nowell uses C major scales in both hands. Take care to make the thumb swing under smoothly and neatly.

English trad.
19th cent.

track 87 Solo

The First Nowell

Andante

Arpeggios and triads

A **triad** is the name given to the chord made by playing the first, third, and fifth notes of a scale: thus a C major triad is made of C, E, and G.

An **arpeggio** extends the triad shape by playing the notes one by one, adding the starting note an octave higher, and then coming down again.

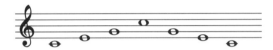

C major arpeggio

To play an arpeggio, the distance between your fingers needs to be wider.

- With your fingers in position over the keys, keeping your hands as relaxed as you can, play the C major arpeggio, each hand in turn.

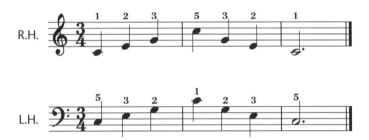

Trumpet Fanfare on the next page uses C major arpeggios and triads. It is mostly marked *forte*: aim for a full, rich, and even tone, rather than a heavy one. The fingering for the right-hand repeated notes in the fourth line is optional, but you might like to try this technique of repeating the same note while changing fingers, which, in this case, gets your hand into position for the next bar.

🔊 **track 88** Solo

Trumpet Fanfare

A. B.

G major scale, arpeggio, and key signature

The scale of G major has exactly the same fingering as C major but starts and ends on G. To maintain the t t s t t t s pattern, the F is sharpened.

- Play the G major scale, each hand in turn:

- Now play the G major arpeggio:

A **key signature** indicates whether sharps and flats are needed throughout a piece, and is found at the beginning of each line:

Thus, this key signature tells you that every F (whatever octave) is to be played as *F sharp*. As we've seen from the scale, this is the key signature of G major.

When we say that a piece is 'in G major' we mean that it is in the *key* of G major: it uses notes from the G major scale for most of the time, and it is likely to end with a G—the key note—as the lowest note in the left hand, and often as the upper note in the right hand as well.

> The first part of the melody of *Plaisir d'amour* was popularized in the mid-twentieth century by Elvis Presley, but it was originally by the German-born composer Martini, who spent most of his life in France writing songs, operas, and military band music. The words begin, 'The pleasures of love last but a moment, but the sorrows of love last a lifetime.'
>
> - It is in G major, so every F is sharpened.
>
> - Occasionally other notes are sharpened too.
>
> - Position your hands well forward so that you can play the black notes with ease and create a smooth-flowing musical line.

track 89 Solo

Plaisir d'amour

J. P. E. Martini
(1741–1816)

F major scale, arpeggio, and key signature

In the scale of F major, the B must be flattened to maintain the t t s t t t s pattern.

The fingering in the left hand is the same as for C and G major, but in the right hand it is different; the thumb goes under after the fourth finger has played B flat.

- To get used to this, play this exercise—practise swinging the thumb under the fourth finger, and back again.

- Repeat the exercise until you are comfortable with this movement.

- Now play the F major scale, each hand in turn.
- Note the key signature, telling you that every B is flattened.

- Now play the F major arpeggio:

Up to now, when you have changed hand position there has been space in the music to move—during a rest or after a staccato note. However, you often need to change position where there appears to be no time to do it, as in the American spiritual *Jubilee* on the next page.

It is important to keep the music in time, not waiting while you find the new hand position. Slightly shorten the note before the change of position to give you time to move; it's a bit like taking a breath when you are singing.

As well as counting steadily in your head, emphasize the dynamic markings in this lively song, to give it colour and character.

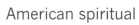track 90 Solo

Jubilee

American spiritual

More about the sustaining pedal

Now that you have used the sustaining pedal in several pieces, you will have noticed that it doesn't only sustain the notes, it also enriches the sound. This is because, by raising the dampers from the strings, it causes all the strings to vibrate in sympathy with the strings actually being played (on the better electronic digital pianos this effect is simulated). So, although there are some pieces where the music moves so quickly that any use of the pedal would blur the sound unpleasantly, in most pieces the pianist's right foot is resting on the pedal, ready for action!

The secret of good pedalling is to listen to your playing critically, so that you can judge when it is appropriate to press the pedal down, and more importantly, when you should lift it up.

In this book we indicate where the pedal should be used, but in much music it is left to the player to decide when and if to use the pedal, with only the most general indications being given (or none at all).

Pedalling exercises

- Keeping your heel on the floor, press the pedal down. Now count 1 2 3 4 repeatedly and steadily, raising the pedal on each '1' and then pressing it down again as soon as you can.

- Make sure that the ball of your foot is always touching the pedal, and make the pedal movements quickly but not jaggedly or forcefully.

This technique is called **legato pedalling**, and the object is for the pedal to be off for just long enough to clear the sound, but no longer. It is often notated with an inverted 'v' to indicate the up and down movement. It will need some practice, but persevere!

- Now play these arpeggios, but using the third finger for every note. You can't make it legato with your fingers, so use legato pedalling to make it smooth, but without making the notes overlap.

- Lift the pedal exactly on the first beat and lower it almost immediately, as soon as the sound has cleared.

- For each exercise, count the pulse steadily.

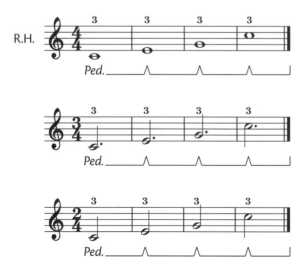

Silent Night was first performed in a version for voice and guitar by its composer at a Bavarian Christmas Night Mass in 1818. Imagine the music echoing round the church and use the pedal to create a rich and peaceful sound.

- Follow the pedal markings carefully and listen to the sound: notice that some sections work well with the pedal for two bars, and other sections sound best with none at all (*senza Ped.*).

- Make sure that the movement of the pedal doesn't distort the rhythm. If it does, practise the exercises on the previous page until the use of the pedal becomes automatic.

Use the same pedal technique in *You and Me* on page 62.

 **track 91** Solo

Silent Night
(Stille Nacht)

Franz Xaver Gruber
(1787–1863)

track 92 Solo

You and Me

A. B.

Melodic building blocks

As you know, the basics of melody are rhythm and pitch. You explored the building of melodic ideas in the call and response sections on earlier pages; now here's an opportunity to develop musical ideas without the CD.

Make up a rhythmic shape such as:

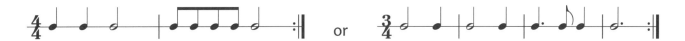

(or choose a rhythm from a piece that you know).

Then add to it a group of notes (playing them in any order, and in any octave that you choose). For example:

You have created a melody; now give it extra colour by incorporating other musical aspects such as:

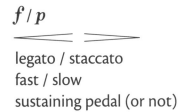

legato / staccato
fast / slow
sustaining pedal (or not)

It might help, too, to think of a mood:

sad / happy
energetic / relaxed
love / hate

Of course you don't have to use only five notes, or limit yourself to one hand—be as adventurous as you like!

More musical signs and Italian terms

Here are some more musical signs and words that you will come across.

8va ┄┄┄┄┄┄┄┄┄┄┄┄┄┄┄┐   *8va* means play the bracketed passage an octave higher.

8vb ┄┄┄┄┄┄┄┄┄┄┄┄┄┄┘   *8vb* or *8va bassa* means play the bracketed passage an octave lower.

⌒ the **pause** (or **fermata**) sign means hold the note or rest over which it is placed for longer. The length for which it is held depends on the context and is up to the player, but somewhere between one-and-a-half times as long and twice as long usually works well.

D.C. or **da capo** (from the head) means go back to the beginning.

D. C. al Fine means go back to the beginning and stop when you get to **Fine** ('the end'). If the piece also has repeat marks, the repeats should be observed only on the first time through.

Sometimes the end of a repeated section is different from the first time. This is shown using **first time bars** and **second time bars**:

Play the bar(s) within the first time bracket the first time, but miss them out the second time and go straight to the second time bracket.

More Italian terms: *espress., espressivo*   expressively
                        cantabile   smoothly, as if singing
                        sim., simile   similarly, in the same way (e.g. for pedal markings)

Drink to me only uses first and second time bars and D.C. al Fine (remember that the first eight bars are played only once when they return at the end). In *Polovtsian Dance* the first time 'bar' is actually three bars, so you should miss all three bars out on the second time round. Note the use of the 8va sign (jump to the new position), and the pause and the 8va bassa sign at the end.

🔘 **track 93** Solo

Drink to me only

English trad.

🔊 **track 94** Solo

Polovtsian Dance

from *Prince Igor*

Alexander Borodin
(1833–87)

Compound time

Up to now, we've used the time signatures $\frac{2}{4}$, $\frac{3}{4}$, and $\frac{4}{4}$. All of these are examples of **simple time**, which means that the beat (crotchets) is divisible by two (quavers).

In **compound time**, the beat is divisible by three. The commonest compound time is $\frac{6}{8}$.

This time signature means that there are six quavers (eighth-notes) in each bar, which are grouped in threes, giving two dotted crotchet beats per bar.

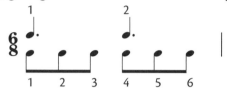

Contrast this with $\frac{3}{4}$, which also contains six quavers, but grouped into three crotchet beats.

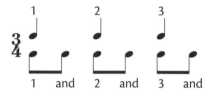

In $\frac{6}{8}$ you will often find the *dotted crotchet rest* (‽) which is worth three quavers.

- Clap or play the following rhythms, counting aloud first.
- You can hear them played on ⊙ **track 95**. The 'count-in' is two bars of quavers.

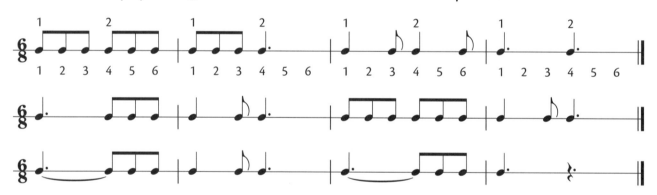

- Now play this tune, again counting carefully.

⊙ **track 96**. The 'count-in' is two bars of dotted crotchets.

Blow the man down   English folk tune

To finish, here are arrangements of three well-known tunes in $\frac{6}{8}$ time: the delicately expressive *O my beloved father*, the calm and reflective *German Cradle Song*, and lastly the traditional song *One More River*—a lively and light-hearted ending to *Pianoworks 1*.

track 97 Solo

O my beloved father

from *Gianni Schicchi*

Giacomo Puccini
(1858–1924)

track 98 Solo

German Cradle Song

Anon.
15th cent. German

track 99 Solo

One More River

Trad.

With humour and bounce

Index

Visual index

OXFORD

Pianoworks
Collection 1

compiled and arranged by
Janet and Alan Bullard

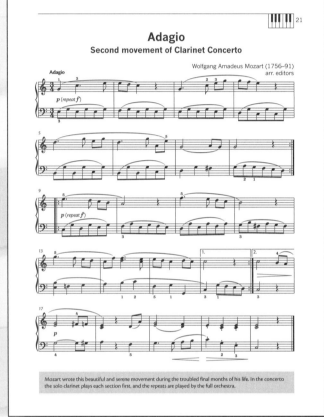

ISBN: 978–019–335583-5

CONTENTS:

✦ Perfect companion to *Pianoworks Book 1*

✦ 30 pieces for beginner pianists

✦ Classical and Romantic favourites, popular songs and show tunes, easy contemporary classical pieces, traditional melodies, Christmas carols, and new works by the authors

✦ Short notes giving tips on style and technique, and informative background information on the pieces

www.oup.com/uk/music

For the older beginner